Even Poetry Gets the Blues
by Jessica Brooke

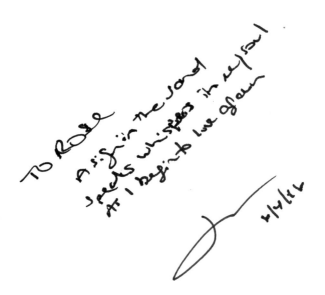

Even Poetry Gets the Blues
by Jessica Brooke

ISBN-13: 978-1482680478
ISBN-10: 1482680475

Dedication

Dedicated to the memory of
Brian Skala, my Nana, Ruth Hartshorn
and my Uncle, Brian Hartshorn
who gave me my gift of poetry.

Acknowledgements

I acknowledge the following people and groups that encouraged, inspired and assisted me in making this collection of my treasured poetry possible. I would like to thank the Free Poets Collective for giving me the opportunity to read my poetry in a welcoming environment. I would like to thank my wonderful mother for her support. I love you mom, with all my heart and soul! Thank you as well to my sister Amy Miller and Matthew Simmons for reading my poetry with the Free at Last Players. To my Aunt and Uncle, Ruth Kandel and Kevan Hartshorn; Thank you for being my second home, for your love and generosity. Also, for your interest in my writing. I love you, thank you for your kindness and I cannot leave out Max, Alex, and Atticus! RIP Yoda. To my best friend Corinne - thank you for being my friend through the darkness. You mean so much to me that words do not justify. Thank you to Philby Fisher for your support and inspiration.

Thank you as well to:

Proofreading - Amy Miller and Philby Fisher
Cover design - LeeAnn Falciani
Inside book layout - Dan Uitti
Author photo - Philby Fisher
Author photo editing - Dave Raider

Table of Contents

Reflection

Jessica Brooke

Cohesive Being

Nonchalantly surfing
Over the view of my
Solidification
Into the strong woman
I am today
A cohesive being
Yet also fragile
I avoided tears today
I did not wish to
Cry over the past anymore
Hurt and stress abound
I just want to exist

Even Poetry Gets the Blues

The sound of our song
Breaks my heart
Just a little bit more
So I sit here and write
Another poem
You will never read
For you sure as hell have
Lost interest in me

As each pen-stroke graces the
Paper with its presence
I remember all of the tears
I shed for you

As a tear would sometimes
Stain the page
Upon which I wrote
Like the tear
Was the poem's tear

I guess poems cry too
Cry for lost loves
Sing for joyful times
Bleed anguish felt by
An image on a screen

Cry for all the times
The poet has writer's block
And misses the pen
Gliding to give the poem its voice
Its life

I guess even poetry gets the blues

Goodbye and I Love You

Cracked and withered
My smile and my heart squeezed
Eyelids forced shut by years
Of rehearsed closing

For maybe if I shut out the screaming
It will just stop
Maybe if my friends really loved me
If a man really ever truly did
Then they wouldn't leave for good

Goodbye is such a fickle word
It can sometimes mean forever
Which in many cases I wish
I never chased after the possibility
That it was only "see you later"

Well see now?
See this smile I taught myself long ago?
I bet you can't spy a shadow so tall
A monster deep as the ravine is wide
A crag, crevice, a hole
In which I hide when
I don't feel like being Jessica anymore

Disassociate and just BE
Survive and (overcome)
Then the suffering may CEASE?

Try appreciating my friendship
For taking a person for granted
That should be a sin in itself
For I do not leave others as easily
As they come in
The door whisks tight
Locks in moonlight

I hear whispers that say
You are leaving again and I am alone
So please just tell everyone
No one's home?

The truth is

I just don't need any more surprises
Phone calls with a reverie
Empty promise or memory
A chalkboard of phrases
Scratched in erasable marker today

So when today becomes tomorrow
Will there be a hello?
Or just another disappointment
A disconnected phone
A machine
A scream
A letter
A disorganized goodbye
Or maybe only a final one

Jessica Brooke

For the finality of the word Goodbye
Is a word Brian heard
It cut him to the quick
So just tell me you love me
Quit the goodbyes

For I am not a quitter
Many are but the one thing
I avoid, yet never quit and DO CHOOSE?

LIFE

Insomniac Ramblings

As night wastes away into oblivion
I contemplate life and reality
Anything to occupy the insomniac
Ramblings through my mind
So a ritard slows down the pattern
In the concerto played so sweetly
And as the moon glows brighter
Through the window's pane
Pain I give myself over to
Emotional and torturous to my core
My being only a plaything to the night
A marionette with cut strings
Listless in a heap in this chair
My cat beckons me to bed
Yet all this humdrum in my head
A cacophony of reasoning resonates
I slowly become tired
Yet fight against the sandman
Dreading only a recurring nightmare
Where nothing can hurt me anymore
Yet still I avoid what so many enjoy
Getting under the silky warm covers
To only wake up refreshed

Letting in the Darkness

Taking a moment given
To have a recollection
Of the most lofty progressions
From my past until now

I was not as strong yet not weak
I never wanted to be perceived
As weak with tears
Even though tears are cleansing
Like having bathed in purity

I could sometimes not cry for months
Yet a simple song or moment
A nuance like a fragrance
Rush forth such a strong response
I am just now getting used to

It is funny what one has to get accustomed to
Undergoing inner turmoil
Putting off sleeping
To inhibit dreaming
Quietly waiting, yet not so patiently

A new beginning
An awakening of repressed memories
Confounding boundaries
Here in silence I sit
It is nighttime and I am strangely calm
Yet my heart beats
Just a little more fiercely
My breathing becomes shallower

I attempt to stop unconscious thoughts
From developing into more
If this was a movie there would
Be one hell of a score
Wanting sleep to come
So daylight comes quicker
Or do I stay awake until
The night goes away?

I think I will just call a friend
To lean on for a bit
Or have a cup of tea
One thing I have to remember to do
Is to rely on myself
No other outside sources
To truly be free

Lifeline

I am ever changing
No one can change me
I survive on a lifeline
I threw myself long ago
In order to carry on

To live life with a closed off mind
Now relishing the fact
There is so much to remember
But to forget is sweet melancholy
Bittersweet forgiveness as well

I feel like crying for your loss
I never liked you to see me cry
So with dry eyes
Standing in the pouring rain

I remind myself it is time to heal
Not time to force myself
To know the past
The past is so far gone
I am a new person
A brand new woman
Brace yourselves
For the ride

Nature

A New Trail

Carefully avoiding exposed
Roots in the forest
As I run

Breathing in the scent
Of the damp, fallen leaves
Underneath my feet

As I am enraptured
By the beauty of autumn
A splendor arises over
The next bend in the trail

A reflection of
The trees upon the lake
Mirroring my contentment
Awakened by the crisp air
Fulfilling my experience

Alone to contemplate
Reflect upon the happenstance
That I stumbled across this trail

Pleased by the fortuitousness
The glory of the experience
Unstoppable and free

Missing the Leaves

In the winter
The trees miss their leaves
Painfully falling after
Growing glorious colors
Barren the trees remain

Until buds form and flowers
Adorn each with fragrance
Color and vibrancy

Naked trees just do not seem
Right to me
Spring will soon come
Bright green leaves will grow
The renewal

Pressed Ink

As the blooming flowers
Press themselves
Upon the page
This ink paints on
Creating a beautiful
Pattern of stems and petals
A mixing of pistils and stamens
Delicate nuances not
Glanced over
A theater for one
As nature meets art

The Seagulls Cry My Name

As the seagulls cry
Over a beach rocky
Yet serene in its emptiness

The peace felt
By toes in the sand
Footprints erased by the
Wake of the waves

As the tide rolls in
The salty sea foam
Brings up a splash to my lips
Palatably pleasing

Bringing a spring smile to my face
As my contentment
Lends to the purity of the moment

The sheer bliss of nature
No replication only appreciation
The seagulls cry my name

Jessica Brooke

Love

Jessica Brooke

A New Love

A cloud of impressions
Fluffy and clear
Overwhelming hope leads me to
A new plane of space where
I haven't laughed so hard or
Smiled so much in so long
I wish I could hug you
Hold your face in my hands as I kiss you
Reveling in bliss under an azure sky
Not an iota of wants and needs
That are more important as you and I

Love Springs

You are my scent
Of springtime
My dew on each
Flower blooming
The crimson color
On the robin's breast
The first crocuses to bloom
In sweet delight
The honeysuckle sweetness
The flowering trees
Fragrance breathed
Deep within
Is how I feel
Whenever I think of you

Jessica Brooke

To My Love

Take your rest before me
Let yourself drift off
Upon my chest
As I stroke your hair
Caress your arms
Feeling closeness
Is a mutual need
Let us start over
Reduce the past
For to end happiness
Is full of regret

Whispers in the Wind

Deciding happiness
Over darkness
Wanting deliverance
As the shadows slip away
As I blow a whisper into the wind
So quietly
"I don't want to be alone"

I want a love that will be forever
Yet now I see that happiness is more than skin deep
I have to love myself outside and in
So blow me a kiss to catch my whisper
Cradle me in my sleep

To brighter dreams
Less scary shadows
I hate desolation
Pain and disorder
Yet I feel positivity
Light and…still disorder
However I am alive and proud to say
I am still here

Jessica Brooke

Sadness

Angel Full of Pain

I am a rare gem
A tricky lovely angel
With a heart full of pain
Hiding deep shame
Relaxing on a hidden pier
My feet in the water
Thinking of the days
I could fly and escape
Now made to accept my fate is excruciating
With no one to help me through
I feel like dying
I am dying inside
Escape sweet escape
In the mirror I can see my sad eyes
Why can no one else see the true real me?
I feel my larynx choked
By years of holding in my voice
The mere sound astounds me
I will get up and go on
Yet misery fills every step
God has given me the strength to stand
But why not be taken by the wind
And how to blow away?

Present Future

Terracotta patterned existence
A muffle in a sea of silence
A chance to feel solace
Amongst strangers
Done waiting for
My future to exist in the present
I fought against truths
By struggling to stay awake
Just wishing once the sun came up
That what I knew
Could give me a bit of respite
Until night fell again

Jessica Brooke

Planted

Why in my deepest darkest moment
Did you leave me desolate and breaking
When I needed you the most you let me down
A so called friend who I could always count on
But then when it got really hard you just left

So please spare me with any reason you have
We have no contact
It tears me inside
To realize I was just too much trouble
You had your own life

I was under lock and key
Banished for months
Forgotten about except
By only one person
Who got me through the toughest times

Then when things went well with him
He blossomed
I realized I loved him
Shattering my heart
Never to hear from him again

My energy unrewarded
Six long years you were gone
I stuck by you
Visited you
Wrote you
Accepted your calls

But now dear
You are only words on a page
Yellowed and stained
Put in a box
Where I keep bad memories

You made me suffer
When I was down and lonely
Why do all good friends
Seem to just leave in the end?
I guess they are not strong enough
To care any longer

Well I am not of that nature
Not of that breed
And to think a relationship blossoms
From just one seed

Jessica Brooke

Silence

I want to be alone with my thoughts
Simple silence
No conversations in my head
No interpretations of water
Sounding like a voice

Frustrated yet not alone
I find help in the
Kindness of others
However there is only
So far I can depend on
Someone else to help

So I choose to be mature
Help myself through it all
I feel like I am going to fall
Flat on my face
An angel fallen from grace

I wish I could still fly
In my dreams and explore
Yet that was my way
To run away
So please silence come
Just be here
If I had one wish right now
It would be to be alone
Inside my head

The Dance of Anxiety

Maybe if I just write it all down
All the anxiety will just go away
Fleeting the feeling is
While I am typing
Or one with my pen
But when night creeps
Its head in
Fear sneaks from every crevice
It is hard to stay sane
When I feel fractured inside
Someone turned the
Light switch off in my heart
All that is left are filaments
All exposed is my emptiness
As anxiety and the night
Dance as one

When Darkness Falls

Fearing dark desolation
Falling upon stones
Sharp and honed
Unwanted melancholy
Overtakes

I find myself passing by
Myself only an onlooker
Please may I get up for air
I am choking on pain
So deep it remains

So passionately I cry out
"Someone save me!"
I ask in vain
But then I realize
Not one of you
Really knows me

My horror or my forgiveness
So take away the anger
The sorrow and laughter
Leave behind all that is empty
All hollowness beside

Take up pieces of me
I wish to keep close
Then burn down the rest
Forever to ash

Dedicated

Jessica Brooke

Angel of True Light ... For Lailah

Angel of pure light
Never doubt your
Place in life
Your kindness knows
No bounds
Your voice
Calms a tempest inside me
Your peaceful demeanor
Speaks of a true soul
Full of love
Who would do anything for another
Sacrificing yourself in the process
Praying for others as I pray for you
I want you to know how much I care
Never doubt I will be there
To cherish your friendship
As much as I am allowed
To give you light when you need it
Even though your radiant wings shine true
Through your eyes horror was witnessed
Yet you persevere
I admire the woman you have become
I aspire to be as kind as you
For I tend to lose my temper
But I find a friend true in you
With no need to yell or fight
For you cast a radiant light

Peace of the Dragons

True love like a clear night
Never wanting to be out of sight
So serene, pure, and true
Not only one lover but two

Gentle kisses and sweet embraces
The glowing smiles on your faces
Pain melting away with a hug
A wish for your anniversary a jug
Of never-ending joy and freedom from pain
A calm feeling like spring rain

Holding hands fast and strong
A love lasting ever so long
A year filled with joy and bliss
So fulfilled with each special kiss

Reminded always with the dragon ring
Earthly angels gather and sing
To forever last
As all this time has passed

So quickly yet with priceless memories
As quiet as a forest of woodland trees
I wish endless love upon you
To grace you both to be forever new

To Amy and Matt upon your one year anniversary!

Petals

I cast my love in the wind
Like so many petals
Lost from the white flowers
Saved since you passed away
Since my heart is broken
I miss you my dear angel Nana
I miss Uncle Brian who became my angel
We all still miss him so
But I know you are with him

I never knew what I would do
If I could no longer call
Hear your voice
Sit around the table with you
Enjoying your fruit salad
I used to try and comprehend
The empty hole in my heart
That is however filled with my love

My longing to see you once again
I know that time will come one day
I will get to hug you again and
Tell you I love you
From the ends of the earth
To the Heavens up above
I give you my love

I feel you here
Your presence comforting me near
I would give anything
To even have a dream of you
To comfort me true
Forever remembered
Never forgotten
God welcomed another angel
That peaceful day on Earth
Where you no longer wished to stay

To Nana

A Happy Triple

A happy couple
Became triple
Completed at last
A journey to find love
Realized and attained

A goal to be united
Is a struggle day to day
Repeated
Yet love overwhelms
The three

Those who are blessed
To know this triplicate
Is honored and supremely lucky

Oh please let the ocean disappear
Only stepping stones
To reach the other side
As if really just a pond

Dedicated

Depression lifted by a smile
A loving song written from the heart
Warming souls who listen
With harmony beyond words

Lead vocals croon of a love so true
Captivated listeners are in awe
No one can put asunder
The loving and caring had for each other

Nothing can erase
The feelings shared and expressed
On pages and pages of love poems
Given freely to one in need
The gift eternal of unconditional love

To Ken, Kristine, and Katharine

Jessica Brooke

To Nana on Your 90th Birthday 6/6/10

Strong willed
With willpower, commitment
Day after day
There is so much
That I can say

A lover of antiques
Gems and jewelry
Plants, chipmunks
Birds, and nature's beauty

Kind, generous
Lovely and true
There are so many reasons
I love you

A caring word to
Brighten my day
There are so many ways
I can convey
All that you mean to me

I hope in every
Hug and smile
You can see
How blessed I feel
That you are part of my life
In times of happiness
And times of strife

I owe so much to you
I don't think you realize
How much you do
To impact my life
Day after day

Here is a little poem for your birthday

A True Soul

Rowdy when she wants to be
Shy and demure when you know her
Truly out for your best interest
Always there when you need her
Caring, true, devoted
Pure of heart
Yet underneath a wild woman
Ready to come out
Running with the wolves

For Corinne

Darkness

Blackness

Anguish and deep sorrow
Cocoon me in aching pain
I have survived this far
However where do I go from here?

I see a gloomy horizon up ahead
I try to step into the light
But the blackness brings me back

I would kiss the ground to have a
Peaceful moment alone on a sunny rock
Away from the brambles and prickers
Blocking the way to the exit
Of the maelstrom inside my brain

Blue Seasons

Blue seasons
Of dark dank depression
Thoughts bring me
To a past I wish to forget
Where locked up
Yet not forgotten

I am experimented on
With pills
Only to stay so long
Because the guinea pig
Is still not getting better
Interns try to learn
I guess I am a good case study
One who goes off and freaks out
When locked in

Freedom
Sweet fresh air
After months of feeling
So alone in the world
With cruel staff

In this life where
I am cursed
To be mentally ill
But that does not mean
I give up

No staying in bed anymore
For there are so many reasons
To live and shine on

43

My Song of Beauty

I sing a song
Of ageless beauty
Brought forth from
Cleansing from within
The deep aching is present

Here attempting to
Drag me down
Into depths I have been before
Heaven and Hell forbid
That I go forth into this race

To love myself and truly feel
Know and say
"I am beautiful"
As darkness descends upon
My quiet bedroom at night

I fear the foreboding
I fear the absence of light
So I fall asleep so it is
Sooner that I reach the light

So Alone

Tear apart my heart
Build a hedge around my soul
Until even when trimmed
No one can get in

For protection is vital
Especially when so much
Power was taken from me
So I rise
Weary and spent

Hoping today will
Be more rewarding
Full of happy experiences
A stranger smiled at me today

I feel alone in a maelstrom of others
While I struggle to maintain my sanity
A wrecking ball had smashed down
My self esteem
Slowly I built it up by sheer will
But alone!
I cannot do all this by myself!

Jessica Brooke

Telling Images

Like snippets
Of microfilm
Tatters of
Macramé friendship bracelets

Remembering happy times yet ones filled with terror
I try hard to focus on the positive
Like others want me to
But I suffer

I suffer oh so much
My smile hides the deep aching knowledge
I seemed so happy
I always had a smile to
Show my friends and I do not want to die
I never even tried
I could have so many times

I want to KNOW for sure what he did
ALL OF IT
Please if there is a God I prayed to
I am figuring there must have been or
I wouldn't be alive now however
Like splinters upon the railing
That stick deep into my skin
Like memories only dust blown away

46

The Gatekeeper

Pervading fear
Leads to pain and isolation
Alone in my head
A cacophony ensues
End the madness
Where the gatekeeper resides
On his whim
The key to freedom
I fight the day to protect me
From the night
I force the night
To be alright
By pills
No solution even works out
God help me
Sort this out

Lost Soul

In the shadows
A mist appears
Awakening the din
Of the creatures
Of the night

Crickets and owls
Chirp and hoot
At the sight of
A fog diffusing
Through the air
Invading their sleep
Foreboding and cold
Silent yet frightening

A green tinge
Is seen from
The nearby cemetery
Where just by chance
A ghostly figure appears
Seemingly alive

Yet the forest awakens
Puts all on high alert
For each evening she walks
Lantern in hand
Trying to find her way

The legend says
She was lost in the woods
One lonely night
Tripped and fell
Into an old well

Boards cracked and broken
Her cries were not heard
She died from exposure
A lantern on the grass
Was her only trace

So cold and alone
Screaming in vain
So she leaves the cemetery
For she is a lost soul
A life ended too short
A life of solace
Yet a life full nonetheless

She misses her lover
Who used to walk the same path
It is now when she visits him
Each evening
The fog a reminder
Of that fateful night
Six years ago

Every night she
Lies next to her lover
Unbeknownst to him
He is never alone

Jessica Brooke

Abuse

Panic

A shallow breath
Begins to speak
A quiet whisper
Becomes a
Thundering shout

A terrified girl
Becomes a
Traumatized woman
Finally verbalizing
Bringing upon
Anxiety, panic, and tears

Vitalizing her spirit
The tears bring back
Her breath
Bring to light
The truth

The reason lying behind
Pain brought to the surface
Finally ready
To face the world
With her tragedy
With her loss
With her anger
With her face covered by her hand
Head down and sobbing
The shock wears off

That saying those words aloud
Was new and frightening
I do not want to begin to know
The rest

Time Capsule

The ascent so daunting
From where I was to here
Now another climb
Necessary made possible
By friends, strength, resolve

Please God shelter me
For I am experiencing a time long ago
That feels in itself a dream
Far removed from what once was

So terrifying
Putting me in survival mode
Literally fight or flight
For I flew in my dreams

Vivid nightmares ended
By a confrontation
In a dream where he was
Shrunken small and for once
I was the bigger one
I had to be stronger
Physically stronger than
My dad
So it became so

Trying to push my door in
I would push it shut with my legs and arms
He would often give up
So vivid
My legs built from running

So healthy yet so thin
You weighed about one hundred
Pounds more than me
Yet I could hold my own
I only cried alone at night
Praying to a God I believed in

Yet He could not fix
What I was going through
Just a millisecond in time
Each piece of memory

But each time you rose from
Your chair
I tumbled down the stairs
I just got up again
Assaulting you verbally
Responding to your perverted comments

Not even my diary knew
Strange, isn't it?
I kept silent
The abuse became a daily routine
I am dissolving into the floor
I just want to disappear

That is what I thought
I am in a better place now
Yet lost in broken memories
Feeling physical pain
That happened long ago

I am feeling for
What seems like the first time
So please do not pity me
Just feel love for me
For I did not have love
From my parents

Only high expectations
Lonely observations
Neglected and missed
Except by Dad
As his scapegoat

Take me away again
I cannot even concentrate
On anything except past memories
So I ground myself

Remind myself where I am
So I can begin to reveal a new me
Proud to let everyone see
The time capsule that is me

Lost Love

Jessica Brooke

Echo

My finite understanding
Of your lack of ability to respect
My feelings, my own needs,
My thoughts
Breaks down
My resolve and dignity
I find myself a shell,
Cavernous and echoing
With my voice that I had
Lost because of you

Jukebox

The disc of tragedy
Plays in the jukebox
Of pain
Songs all too familiar
Conquer to torture me
Endlessly
It is funny how powerful
Music is
How it can put me in a place
With someone and many times
I ache every time the song plays
Also repeatedly in my brain
The memory of you remains

Breaking Up

A part of me is breaking down
I do not know where to find resolve
A deep gnawing feeling of an ending and a loss
Brings to the forefront
What I always dread when it comes to pass
A bit of my heart taken

Spurned

Taking in a moment
To reverse the present
Further back
Until I had never met you
For to spurn another
Only to tease me
Is a sacrilege to love

What You Missed

You do not know what you missed
When you left me you passed up
A gifted poet, romantic lover
A talented and intelligent woman
A dancer, a singer, your best friend
A great listener and not to mention
Beautiful and sweet inside and out

You do not know what you missed
You missed out on my successes
You missed out on my tears
That you could have dried
You missed out on laughter and excitement
A healthier me

You do not know what you missed
I will find another love
No this love will not be
Anything like you
For I will stop waiting
For someone to live up to the
Standards of our relationship
For this new lover will not
Use me once it is over
For it will not be over

You do not know what you missed
That's your loss and clearly not mine
Yes I remember happy times
Nothing is always sugar and roses
However now I know
I deserve better than what
Even you could give me
I am healthier now and no it is
Not because of you
For you chose to shut me out

You do not know what you missed

Jessica Brooke

Whispers

Take apart the damage
You have done
Consolidate into a conglomerate
Of whispers confessing love
Love that you said you lost for me
I still hold you deeply to my heart

Set me free
Angels of sweet mercy
As I swing from a decaying tree
Snapping branches
Falling
Stapled to the ground

I cannot spare myself the heartache
I try to say I do not think of you
I wonder if you do for me?
I want to know what the future
Holds in her pristine hand for me

I guess I am meant to be lost
Until someday
My solitary self
Finds love again

Hope

Jessica Brooke

Dreaming Into Being

Stepping away
Being taken aback
By who I am now
A huge turnaround
Of years ago
No longer homeless
But hopeful
No longer dreaming
But being
Finding time to just
Be myself
As the second hand
Hits the twelve
Another minute has
Come and gone
I must not waste the day
There is happiness in store
I just constantly remind myself
That I want something more

Dust Storm

A dark dreary dust storm
Comes to ruin with disorder
A life so full of hope

Yet only fleeting winds
Gust and echoes of the
Past are whispered

Quickly then dissipating
As the night falls
The moon is seen after the din

A glow brighter than
Previously ever seen
Please moon light my path

Through the wreckage of
My past now destroyed
Leaving in its wake

A new start

Jessica Brooke

Self-Improvement

As the "demons" exit my mind
I exert my thoughts elsewhere
To what I may like to improve
About myself or my life

Of course there are so many
I am working towards some goals
Some are being realized
Others are hard work attained
Sometimes

Patience is a big quality
I would love to possess
I would like to stop arguing
With my family
I would like to lose more weight

However on the inside
I am a delicate flower
Just waiting for its chance to bud
For a fragrance to waft out
Into every room I step in

Such that everyone notices
Or maybe only one special person
Whom I have waited for
I do not know his name
Or what he looks like
But others say he is out there

I feel horrible I have to let down
Those that pledge their love to me
But I cannot change my standards
I cannot change my feelings
Or lack thereof
It hurts my heart to tell them so
But I will know when THE ONE comes along

Still a work in progress
Under construction
Is my self-love
So that I may be able to
Share my heart and mind with another
Maybe also find someone
That will not pressure me
In more ways than the obvious

I hear stories of my friends
Their relationships

Feelings of jealousy
Wistfulness and remembrance
Of days filled with joy
Someday…

Jessica Brooke

Sun on My Heart

A slave to my own mistakes
A walking conundrum with a conscience
In love with nature
Yet apprehensive to go outside

Vacant emptiness is filled by smiles of friendship
Give me a hand to hold on to
For I have lost my grip on love

The car I am driving in is going nowhere
A vehicle in transit only to find
A series of one-way streets
An impasse to my success

I have tempted success many times but failed
With each tease of better days
There exists doubt and turmoil
Where my brain is my worst enemy

I need to find confidence in a sea of failures
Let the sun shine on my heart
My body is open to the warmth of another soul
I will not let past failures get me down
For every time I was knocked down I just GOT UP

The Fog

The fog of insecurity
Rolls in
Blanketing my resolve and dignity in limbo
I try to breathe and I am extinguished
By the dense, thick, smoke-like clouds

However if I think about it
I am amongst the clouds
Without even being up high
Then a new realization is attained

That I don't have to always be perfect
Or in control when I can sometimes be
In a haze created by nature
Never alone in my heartache
With a friend to lean on

Even when the night pervades the light
I feel negativity and fear
I shall relax and let myself rest
Until the dawn brings clear sun

Jessica Brooke

The Self Confident Crew

I do not know what else to do
I spend time attempting to love myself
When I think falsely that I have
Achieved such an ascent

A scent of success moves within
I feel accomplishment in my life
I am a perfectionist
So nothing is ever good enough

I guess I truly do feel that way
But the sun gives me great hope
Happiness that I am a survivor
That I woke up to greet another day

Sometimes I wish the day would be over
Just to move on to the next
Please just let me in
I am kind and giving

Let me in to the self confident crew
Always smiling although you
Never know if it is a real smile
The so called perfect happy people
Could be unhappy with misery inside
Just like I was

So I cannot compare myself to others
Feeling jealous of what they have
Instead of appreciating and celebrating
What I DO have
Even though it is not romantic love

I do have friendship
I have my poetry
I have pets that need and love me
I have a roof over my head
I have clothes to wear
I have food in my freezer
It is staggering how upsetting it is
To be homeless

Jessica Brooke

I appreciate what I have
Just a bit more than others
For I was homeless
I had no friends
No pets
No safe place to go
No refuge but my car

So tell me again
Myself
"Why do you not love yourself?"
Well it was instilled in me
That I was ugly
Worthless and I was so alone

I have forgiven, with no anger
Hate was such a weight to bear
Baring my soul on the page
Is the only way I know how
To let out all the darkest turmoil

Thanks for reading
My inner ramblings

Thank you for being loyal
To my pen

Trifles and Spontaneity

When I don't have to think of
Unnecessary trifles
Just live life on a whim
With spontaneous abandon
I realize that the moment
Is best to live in instead
Of the past

For I will find a calmer and deeper
Present and future that
I cannot always find living
When aching pervaded my life
I wish to make someone smile
Every day

I resolve to be more giving
Realizing I do already but there
Can always be more kindness
In a world of everything but
So it seems

Yet I find most often a day
That someone made a deep impact
Upon my life so that I could
Take with me that gift
And "sleep on it" to bring me
A brighter tomorrow

Jessica Brooke

Warrior

I am at the pinnacle
A warrior with pride
Pride in my battle scars
My wounds healed
My smile brighter

I stand upon lofty heights
Wishing always for more
Yet I separate myself
From then and now
She is someone else
I have shed her skin

I do not know her anymore
I only know that when I
Look at myself in the mirror
I see a strong, determined woman
Not a scared teenager
Or roughed up girl

I know where I came from
My roots were ripped up
So long ago
On my own and winging it
Through life

Now my wings are unfurled
I am ready to fly
Feeling free and lessening pain
I sit here forever and remain
Myself

I did not change for anyone else
Except me
If you do not like whom I have become
Keep walking

Jessica Brooke

When Up Turns Downward

Thoughts compounding
Overwhelming
Where to turn?

Dark pervading
However resolve
Keeps me going

Strength to overcome
Any downfall
Yet when up turns downward

My life seems
To have the doldrums
Boring constant days
That just roll on by

Yet a hug from a friend
Brings me back to the
Deepest part of my heart...LOVE

Made in the USA
Middletown, DE
18 May 2016